LAB series

GEOLOGY LAB
FOR KIDS

Rocking Out with Rocks

EXPLORING THE WONDERS OF IGNEOUS, SEDIMENTARY, AND METAMORPHIC ROCKS

GARRET ROMAINE

QUARRY

Brimming with creative inspiration, how-to projects, and useful information to enrich your everyday life, Quarto Knows is a favorite destination for those pursuing their interests and passions. Visit our site and dig deeper with our books into your area of interest: Quarto Creates, Quarto Cooks, Quarto Homes, Quarto Lives, Quarto Drives, Quarto Explores, Quarto Gifts, or Quarto Kids.

© 2018 Quarto Publishing Group USA Inc.
Text © 2017 Garret Romaine
Photography © 2017 Quarto Publishing Group USA Inc.

First Published in 2018 by Quarry Books, an imprint of The Quarto Group,
100 Cummings Center, Suite 265-D, Beverly, MA 01915, USA.
T (978) 282-9590 F (978) 283-2742 QuartoKnows.com

All rights reserved. No part of this book may be reproduced in any form without written permission of the copyright owners. All images in this book have been reproduced with the knowledge and prior consent of the artists concerned, and no responsibility is accepted by producer, publisher, or printer for any infringement of copyright or otherwise, arising from the contents of this publication. Every effort has been made to ensure that credits accurately comply with information supplied. We apologize for any inaccuracies that may have occurred and will resolve inaccurate or missing information in a subsequent reprinting of the book.

Quarry Books titles are also available at discount for retail, wholesale, promotional, and bulk purchase. For details, contact the Special Sales Manager by email at specialsales@quarto.com or by mail at The Quarto Group, Attn: Special Sales Manager, 401 Second Avenue North, Suite 310, Minneapolis, MN 55401, USA.

10 9 8 7 6 5 4 3 2 1

ISBN: 978-1-63159-456-4

Digital edition published in 2018

Content for this book was originally found in *Geology Lab for Kids* by Garret Romaine (Quarry Books, 2017).

Page Layout: Alex Youngblood
Photography: Patrick Smith Photography, except images by Shutterstock on cover, right bottom, and page 15.

Printed in USA

CONTENTS

Introduction 4
Identifying Rocks and Minerals 6

UNIT 1
LIVING WITH LAVA 8

Lab 1: Volcanic Action 9
Lab 2: Intriguing Intrusions 11
Lab 3: Lovely Lava Cakes 13
Lab 4: Cocoa Crust 15

UNIT 2
SUPER SEDIMENTS 17

Lab 5: Fun with Mud 18
Lab 6: Settling Sediment 20
Lab 7: Tasty Conglomerate 22

UNIT 3
MAJOR METAMORPHOSIS 24

Lab 8: Smears of Pudding 25
Lab 9: Snaky Schist 27
Lab 10: Chocolate Rock Cycle 29

Resources 31

About the Author and Acknowledgements 32

INTRODUCTION

Geology is the science of the Earth and learning to describe what you see so that someone else can understand. Once you get good at talking about the world around you, it's not hard to take that to the next level and figure out what happened to the Earth in the past, even if you can't see it happening today. Nobody has ever traveled to the middle of the Earth, but by making models based on places we have been, we think we know what's going on there. That's science—make a prediction, see if you can prove it, and then apply it to bigger questions.

In this book, you will learn a lot about the way things happen and why. You'll be introduced to the science behind processes you see all around you, and you'll learn to think about the Earth in new and exciting ways. Some of the most important parts of geology come down to very simple concepts—gravity, friction, heat, and water.

Geology is based on observations and predictions that are part of the scientific model. Fortunately, the Earth works in a way we can understand, so if we can make the right model, we can use what we see in that model to predict other forces. We can measure things at a small scale, and we can make models to teach others. Even simple, fun projects can show the larger world at work. The labs and projects in this book will help you understand how much fun it is to learn about the world around you.

Over the years, I have spent countless hours working with kids just like you in lectures, at demonstrations, and even as a merit badge counselor, helping them understand the world around them. Many of the labs here are time-tested, having been around for years. But some are completely new or bring a new twist to an old idea. We'll start with simple concepts and then connect the dots to bigger ideas. In that way, these labs are like building blocks: start small and keep building. At some point, you'll probably find that you are learning how more and more pieces of the puzzle fit together. That's always been the most enjoyable for me, showing others how all the different things they already know can apply. It's always a lot of fun to go to the beach and pick up a few rocks, but when you know how to identify the rocks and explain how they got there, you feel like a great detective solving a big riddle. Some of you may even go on to careers in the Earth sciences or become planetary scientists who travel to distant locales. I hope that's the case!

Let's get started. And remember: No one likes a messy lab partner!

IDENTIFYING ROCKS AND MINERALS

Rocks and minerals are the building blocks of the Earth. Minerals have a chemical formula, with an exact number of atoms of different elements. For example, calcite is $CaCO_3$—it has one calcium atom, one carbon atom, and three oxygen atoms. Minerals can be identified with tests for streak, hardness, crystal angle, and density, which you will learn in these labs. Rocks are made up of different minerals, in lots of combinations, and they can be glued, pressed, or melted together in many ways. To identify rocks, you need to know what minerals are in them, how they are held together, and how they formed. You will also learn about the three "families" of rocks: sedimentary, igneous, and metamorphic.

Shown here are many of the most common minerals that you can find, plus a few that are rare and valuable. Most of the rocks listed here are very common. If you can learn to identify them, you can start to explain the world around you.

Minerals

Calcite

Epidote

Feldspar

Fluorite

Garnet

Gold

Gypsum

Jade

Malachite

Muscovite mica

Pyrite

Quartz

Rocks

 Agate
 Basalt
 Chalcedony
 Chert
 Conglomerate

 Gneiss
 Granite
 Jasper
 Limestone
 Marble

 Meteorite
 Mudstone
 Obsidian
 Opal
 Petrified wood

 Quartzite
 Rhyolite
 Sandstone
 Schist

UNIT 1

LIVING WITH LAVA

The Earth uses minerals to create new rocks. Igneous rocks are the most dramatic way the Earth builds up its crust, usually in the form of lava flows and ash clouds. Geologists refer to lava as an *extrusive* rock, because it moved from inside the Earth to outside. Thus, extrusive rocks came out of the Earth. We'll talk later about the other kind of igneous rock, *intrusive* rocks that cool before they erupt from inside the Earth.

There are three main kinds of lava: basaltic, andesitic, and rhyolitic. *Basaltic* lava can be runny and form long flows that cover hundreds of miles or fill in gullies and valleys and end up several hundred feet thick. *Andesitic* lava tends to build up mountains, like in the Andes chain of South America. *Rhyolitic* lava is sometimes explosive, forming dangerous eruptions. All three help build up the Earth, but at this stage, you can use the term *lava* to mean simply "hot, flowing rock."

In these labs, we'll look a little closer at igneous rocks and learn moreabout their features.

VOLCANIC ACTION

The traditional volcano lab involves baking soda and vinegar, but that's not really a geology lab; it's a chemistry lab. In this experiment, you'll build your volcano the old-fashioned way: one lava flow at a time.

MATERIALS

- Small paper flower pot with a hole on top
- Several bottles of white glue or bottles of colored 3-D fabric paint
- Food coloring

Safety Tips

- Don't get glue in your eyes, in your hair, or on your clothes.
- Don't squeeze the glue bottle too hard or you'll have a *real* eruption!

PROTOCOL

STEP 1: Select a paper flower pot with a hole in the bottom. You can arrange it on a board or piece of cardboard when you finish. You can use other forms for your mountain, such as Styrofoam shapes.

STEP 2: Prepare your lava sources (glue or 3-D fabric paint). If you are using white school glue, open the bottles and squirt a bit out. Then mix in plenty of food coloring and stir or shake it up. Try to get at least three different colors for your lava. They can be realistic (dark brown, black, and gray) or a rainbow of colors.

STEP 3: Take turns reaching under the cone and squirting out lava from *inside* the flower pot, so that it flows down the flanks of the volcano, just like a lava flow. Let each flow dry for a few minutes before adding the next layer so they don't mix.

STEP 4: Work your way around and make sure the mountain is covered very well. When it starts to get messy, you can simply drip your flows from the top.

Creative Enrichment

1. You can add some water to one of your glues to make it runnier.
2. If you want your mountain to look more realistic, try adding modeling clay or plaster of Paris to make a good crater at the top before you start.

THE SCIENCE BEHIND THE FUN

Volcanoes are the best understood source of igneous rocks. The 1980 eruption of Mt. St. Helens did not show us very much lava. Instead, it erupted with a giant ash cloud, as the lava inside rushed up and mixed with air too quickly to form puddles of hot lava. This happens more often than you think, and these explosive eruptions are very dangerous. Volcanologists—geologists who study volcanoes—call these kinds of mountains *stratovolcanoes*. These are usually snow-capped, nicely shaped, and pretty to look at, such as Mt. Fuji in Japan or Mt. Shasta in California.

Usually we get big lava flows from what's called a *shield volcano*, such as those in Hawaii. Hot lava pours out of these volcanoes in flows that sometimes go on for years, creeping along the ground and burning up everything in their path. Did you know that it is against the law around the world to try to interfere with a lava flow by building trenches, walls, or dams?

Other types of volcanoes that give us lava are called *cinder volcanoes*. They throw out a lot of ash and cinders, and build up a cinder cone. They are usually smaller and may build up on the slopes of a bigger volcano. Cinder cones also tend to come in clusters, with numerous little buttes and cones in a group.

LAB 2: INTRIGUING INTRUSIONS

This experiment shows how granite rises. When lava doesn't break through the Earth's surface, it cools slowly. We'll see how that intrusion gradually rises over time, like you would see in a lava lamp.

MATERIALS

- 1-pint (473 ml) wide-mouth glass Mason jar (or a drinking glass will work)
- 1 cup (235 ml) of water, room temperature
- Food coloring (optional)
- ¼ cup (60 ml) of inexpensive vegetable oil
- 1 teaspoon of salt (big, coarse rock salt works great)

 Safety Tips
- Avoid getting salt into your eyes.
- Don't knock over your jar.

PROTOCOL

STEP 1: Add 1 cup (235 ml) of water to your Mason jar.

STEP 2: Add four or five drops of food coloring and stir it in. This is optional, but it helps you see what's going on.

STEP 3: Add the oil into the jar. As you probably know, oil floats on top of water.

STEP 4: Sprinkle the salt into your mixture. It should drop to the bottom.

Creative Enrichment

1. Can you guess how much salt you could add before the mixture becomes super-saturated?

2. Does it matter what kind of oil you use?

THE SCIENCE BEHIND THE FUN

This simple take on a "lava lamp" is a little different from the original. The original uses a heat source that melts wax, which rises, cools, falls, and recycles itself. Other forms of this experiment use a lot more oil and effervescent tablets, such as Alka Seltzer, instead of salt. But they work on the same principle. There is a difference between the specific density of water and the specific density of vegetable oil. Most cooking oils measure about 0.92 g/cm^3. Pure water is defined as 1.0 g/cm^3. Since lighter fluids float on heavier fluids, the oil floats on top.

As you added the salt, it captured some oil on its way through the oil layer. This is because the surface tension of oil is high, so it wants to coat things, which you see as the mass drops through the oil. Once the salt reaches the bottom of the container, it starts to dissolve into the water, and as it dissolves, it releases the oil it captured. The oil then wants to rise above the water, and does so as an interesting bubble.

The difference in density is the same process that intrusions use to rise through the Earth's crust. They are a little less dense than the material they are in, and hotter, so they rise slowly. Sometimes there may not be enough difference between the intrusion and the surrounding rock, so the hot magma eventually hardens in place, well below the surface. After a million years of erosion, or thanks to a continued push below, the granite eventually begins to poke out and form mountains.

LAB 3: LOVELY LAVA CAKES

In this lab, you will mimic what happens to a lava flow when it cools.

MATERIALS

- ½ cup (112 g) of butter
- 4 small custard cups
- Baking sheet
- Package of semi-sweet baking chocolate
- 1 cup (125 g) of powdered sugar
- 2 egg yolks—you might need help with this!
- 2 whole eggs
- 6 tablespoons (47 g) of flour
- ½ cup (30 g) of thawed whipped cream dessert topping, such as Cool Whip (or ice cream)

PROTOCOL

STEP 1: Pre-heat your oven to 425°F (220°C).

STEP 2: Smear some (not all) butter around 4 small custard cups and place on a baking sheet.

STEP 3: Microwave the chocolate and remaining butter in a medium microwave-safe bowl for 1 minute, or until butter melts. Stir in powdered sugar, egg yolks, and whole eggs. Mix well.

STEP 4: Add flour. Mix well.

STEP 5: Spoon the batter into your custard cups.

STEP 6: Bake for thirteen to fourteen minutes, until the edges of the dessert are firm. Remove from heat and let stand for one minute.

STEP 7: Run a knife around the edges to break the dessert free, and place them on individual plates. Many recipes call for you to turn the dessert upside down, but for this lab, don't do that. Don't sprinkle more powdered sugar on the top, either. Test the top of the crust just before you dive in—preferably while still hot—with the whipped cream. It should be like the top of a lava flow where the rock has cooled a little.

Safety Tips

- Be careful around the hot oven.

- Ask an adult for help using the oven.

- This recipe involves a microwave and oven instead of a hot stove, but you still need to be careful with hot food and surfaces.

- Don't burn your tongue by digging out the "lava" in the center too soon after it comes out of the oven!

Creative Enrichment

1. Leave in a little longer to get the tops nice and crispy, like a real lava flow.

THE SCIENCE BEHIND THE FUN

These lava cakes show you what a real lava flow looks like, and why they are so dangerous: the top might look firm and hard, but the middle can still be hot and liquid. Unlucky tourists all around the world have been known to get too close to lava flows; the brittle crust breaks under their feet, leading to a fatal conclusion.

If you got the top of the cake nice and crispy, you should notice that it is quite a bit different in color and texture from the cake. That's because heat has almost turned the top of the lava cake to a cinder.

The geological term for that crispy top matter on a lava flow is *scoria*. It is usually full of holes and, in some lava flows, it may even contain little crystals of feldspar.

Scoria is different from *pumice*, a volcanic rock you may already know. Pumice floats on water and is much less dense. Scoria will sink.

Lava cakes are almost like a soufflé, and they may collapse when they cool.

LAB 4

COCOA CRUST

Instead of just making hot cocoa on a cold winter day, make a model of how the Earth's crust moves around thanks to heat from inside the planet.

MATERIALS

- 1-quart (1 L) of heavy cream
- Medium cooking pot
- 1 cup (86 g) of powdered cocoa

 Safety Tips
- Be cautious around the cooking stove to avoid burns.
- Ask an adult for help using the stove.

PROTOCOL

STEP 1: Pour the heavy cream into a medium cooking pot.

STEP 2: Cover the cream with a layer of cocoa, the thicker the better—close to ¼" (6 mm). Make the edges around the pan walls slightly thicker. You just created a model of a "super-continent."

STEP 3: Turn on the heat and slowly bring the cream to a boil.

STEP 4: Watch where cracks form as the system gets hotter, and imagine how many earthquakes you could feel if you were standing on such a piece of the crust. See if you can predict which cracks will grow the biggest.

STEP 5: Keep heating, and avoid the temptation to stir. By the end of the experiment, you may be down to one remaining "island" of crust.

STEP 6: Don't waste the ingredients! Add a little sugar to make hot chocolate.

 Creative Enrichment

1. What happens if you make the chocolate layer ½" (1 cm) thick? Or use instant hot cocoa mix?

2. What happens if you use milk instead of cream?

THE SCIENCE BEHIND THE FUN

The interior of our planet is very hot—probably over 9,032°F (5,000°C) at the inner core, and ranging from 2,912°F to 6,692°F (1,600°C to 3,700°C) in the mantle. With all that heat and pressure, the rocks in the mantle don't behave much like rocks; they're more like plastic or toothpaste. That heat at the core of the Earth must go somewhere, and scientists believe it swirls around in currents through the mantle, just like the heat from the stove moved the heavy cream around.

As the heat increases, the currents in the cream scrape away at the chocolate layer that represents the Earth's crust, and finally, you saw cracks begin. Wherever the crust was thin, the boiling cream found the weakness. At the end, you might see the "plates" start to rock as the heat shifts them. At the Earth's surface, there are several rift zones where the rocks are pulling away from each other. These are *divergent* boundaries or zones where the crust is expanding. You saw a "triple junction" where there were three lines of weakness and, eventually, the cream broke through. Imagine that being a small shield volcano if the cocoa layer was hard enough for the cream to build up.

The theory of continental drift, also called plate tectonics, was first advanced by Dr. Alfred Wegener in 1912. However, it wasn't accepted until the 1960s.

UNIT 2

SUPER SEDIMENTS

While igneous rocks can form in spectacular ways, most of the Earth's crust is covered with sedimentary rocks. Sedimentary rocks are named for the tiny bits of rock and mud—sediments—that build up when material settles out of water, including giant freshwater lakes, rivers, active bays, lagoons, and straits in the ocean. Sometimes the water is muddy, and over the years, layers of silt may settle out in a bay. Over lots of time, that *mudstone* can build up to thousands of feet or meters. Or a river may empty into the ocean and bring in lots of sand and rocks, creating *sandstone*. Elsewhere, a body of water may be carrying lime (calcium carbonate), building up until the water simply can't absorb any more chemicals. At that point, a *limestone* may start forming.

In this unit, we'll look at how sedimentary rocks get started and investigate some special forms of sedimentary rocks.

LAB 5

FUN WITH MUD

It may look like dirty water, but you'd be surprised how much is floating in there.

MATERIALS

- 1-quart (1 L) of soil, dug from the garden—don't use store-bought potting soil
- Bucket and shovel
- Lab notebook and pen or pencil
- Scale (optional)
- Large, wide-mouth jar with lid
- 1-quart (1 L) of water
- Long stick or paint mixer (optional)
- Screen or strainer (optional)
- Set of bowls (optional)

 Safety Tips

- Avoid spills.
- Be careful where you dig to get your soil sample. Get permission first.

PROTOCOL

STEP 1: Collect your soil sample. Record the experience in your lab book: what you did, what colors you saw, how hard was it to shovel out, etc. You can find the weight of your sample by weighing the empty bucket first, then the bucket with soil, and subtracting the bucket's weight to find the final weight.

STEP 2: Fill your jar halfway with the soil you collected.

STEP 3: Add water almost to the top of the jar and put the lid on.

STEP 4: Shake up the jar and break up the clumps. You might want to take the lid off and reach in with a long stick to help things along. A long wooden stick used to mix paint works.

STEP 5: Return the lid and shake it up some more, then let it settle overnight. When you return, make notes about what you see. How did the material settle?

 Creative Enrichment

1. If you have a set of screens with big and little holes, keep going in this lab by dumping the contents into a tub and separating out the material. Put sticks, leaves, and other organic material in a container and put big rocks in another. Then measure out how much sand and clay you have and calculate the ratios.

2. Try the lab again, using a soil sample from another location.

3. Save some of your soil sample for the Settling Sediment lab.

THE SCIENCE BEHIND THE FUN

Soil types depend on how much sand, clay, and organic material is present. Soil scientists do not use the word *dirt*. They either use the word *soil* or they use even more precise terms, like sandy loam and *alluvium*. By noting how much of each main ingredient is present, scientists can tell gardeners and farmers how to treat their soil with the right fertilizer. One tool they use is the Silt-Sand-Clay triangle, based on those ratios.

Chances are you didn't find many big rocks because gardeners like to remove them. Was there very much sand in your sample? Usually there is, and you can divide up the sand particles into fine, very fine, coarse, and very coarse. Measuring the size of the sand is usually something you need many specialized screens for, but it is an important thing to know if you are a soil scientist. The first scale for classifying sediment sizes was developed by American sedimentary scientist J.A. Udden, and was adapted by C.K. Wentworth in 1922.

SEDIMENT SIZES	
Type	**Size**
Clay	0.0001–0.002 mm
Silt	0.002–0.05 mm
Sand	0.05–2 mm
Granule	2–4 mm ($^8/_{100}$"–$^2/_{10}$")
Pebble	4–64 mm ($^2/_{10}$"–2½")
Cobble	64–256 mm (2½"–10")
Boulder	256 mm (10")

LAB 6
SETTLING SEDIMENT

This lab shows how very fine silt and clay settles out until the water becomes clear again.

MATERIALS

- Soil sample (you can use your Fun with Mud sample if you have it)
- 3 large, wide-mouth Mason jars
- Water
- Screen (optional)
- Coin
- Lab notebook and pen or pencil
- Spoon

Safety Tips
- Avoid making a mess.

PROTOCOL

STEP 1: If you still have the soil sample from the Fun with Mud lab, you can use it here. Or you can get another sample. Place it in a jar and fill halfway with water.

STEP 2: Pour only the muddy water into the second jar. If someone holds a screen you can be sure to keep out big pieces of sand and rock.

STEP 3: Place a coin inside your third glass jar and pour in the "dirty water" sample you just made until you are almost to the top of the glass jar. Leave the lid off and allow for evaporation.

STEP 4: Write down your observations. What color is the water? Can you see the coin?

STEP 5: Over the next several hours and days, record more observations. You can use a camera to record each step. If the coin is still showing, you can prepare another "dirty water" sample and pour it in slowly; try not to disturb the sediments that have already settled out. You can do this by pouring your dirty water onto the back of a spoon held just above the surface of the water.

 Creative Enrichment

1. Use a seashell to show how sedimentation can help make a fossil.

2. How many days does it take for the water to clear completely? Is the coin covered?

3. If you let the sample dry out completely, you might be able to pretend you are a fossil preparation expert and dig out the fossil from the dried mud.

THE SCIENCE BEHIND THE FUN

Sedimentation like in this lab occurs in many ocean bays and lagoons all over the world. There are three main kinds of sediment:

- **Clastic:** pieces of rocks and minerals and mostly sand and silt

- **Chemical:** different minerals that are suspended. When sea water is super-saturated it can no longer hold any more salt, and the rest begins to fall to the bottom.

- **Biochemical:** Many forms of sea life create shells to protect themselves. When they die, their shells sink to the bottom of the ocean, forming a calcium carbonate mud. The most common biochemical rock is limestone.

Since 70 percent of the Earth's surface is covered by water, there are a lot of sedimentary rocks formed by sediment sinking to the bottom. Over time, those muds and silts build up, and the weight of the water above them can squeeze them together. In the case of an inland sea, thousands of feet of sediment could build up over millions of years, but then earthquakes might drain out all that water, leaving only the hardened mud rocks behind. In other cases, land that used to be at the bottom of the sea could rise thanks to the way the plates of the crust move around. At some point, all those sediments would be left high and dry. What other ways can sediments at the bottom of the ocean become mountains?

LAB 7
TASTY CONGLOMERATE

Make sedimentary rocks with your favorite ingredients. This is a *conglomerate*—a collection of bits and pieces of material, all glued together.

MATERIALS

- Mixing bowl
- 2 cups (312 g) of oats
- 1 cup (25 g) of puffed rice cereal, such as Rice Krispies
- ½ cup (50 g) of pretzels, chopped up
- ¼ cup (42 g) of tiny shell-covered chocolates, such as M&M's Minis
- Medium saucepan
- ¼ cup (55g) of butter
- ¼ cup (85 g) of honey
- ¼ cup (65 g) of creamy peanut butter
- ¼ cup (60 g) of brown sugar
- Wooden spoon or firm rubber spatula
- 1 teaspoon (5 ml) of vanilla extract
- Glass baking dish
- Parchment paper

 ### Safety Tips

- Be careful with glass mixing bowls.
- Ask an adult for help using the stove.

PROTOCOL

STEP 1: In a large bowl, mix your oats, puffed rice, pretzels, and mini candies. Note that the ingredients list can vary depending on what you like—you can substitute cashews, raisins, chocolate chips, bigger candies, etc. Just keep the proportions about the same. This mixture will be your *clasts*.

STEP 2: In a medium saucepan, melt the "glue" for your conglomerate. Add the butter, honey, peanut butter, and brown sugar and bring it to a boil. Stir continuously so it doesn't stick. Reduce the heat and let it simmer for three minutes and keep stirring. Remove from the heat and add the vanilla.

STEP 3: Add the glue, or *matrix*, to your clasts in the large mixing bowl and stir together until you have everything distributed throughout the mixture.

STEP 4: Line the glass baking dish with parchment paper and add your mixture. Pack it down with your wooden spoon or rubber spatula so that it is nice and flat and even. You can add more candy, raisins, nuts, etc., at this point, either sprinkling them on top or pushing them in slightly.

STEP 5: Put in the refrigerator for about ten minutes, then remove and cut into squares or rectangles. Enjoy!

 Creative Enrichment

1. Is it possible to have too many pieces of candy?

THE SCIENCE BEHIND THE FUN

Conglomerates are common sedimentary rocks. They are usually composed of rounded pebbles of various sizes but at least 2 mm ($8/100$") in diameter or else they're just coarse sandstone. Sometimes conglomerates are glued together with such a hard, lime-rich matrix that they are very hard to break apart. Other times, they have more rocky material (clasts) than they do matrix, and crumble apart easily.

It takes very strong water current to move big rocks, and the size of the rocks in a conglomerate tells geologists about where the conglomerate was made. If the pebbles and cobbles are not very eroded, they will still have sharp angles and corners, and the resulting rock is called a *breccia*. This usually means that the rocks have not traveled very far, and the water current when they were laid down was not very strong.

Gold miners often have to break up conglomerates to wash the gold out. Generally, the bigger the rocks in a stream, the bigger the gold. Conglomerates with large rocks in gold country are often a good sign!

UNIT 3

MAJOR METAMORPHOSIS

In the labs so far, we have learned about the two main ways that new rocks form, through fire and water. But there is a third type of rock: *metamorphic*. These rocks start out as a volcano or a sediment, but undergo so much "cooking" deep inside the Earth that they change, sometimes in profound and interesting ways.

In deep gold mines around the world, miners battle with the heat that increases as they dig lower and lower. We can only imagine what life is like for a crystal when it's buried under 20 miles (32 km) of heavy rock and heated up hotter than a pizza oven. We do know that under those conditions, crystals not only bend, twist, and fold, but they also change their chemistry. Crystals could slowly form under the right conditions of temperature and abundance. Things get even more interesting when you add pressure into the mix.

LAB 8
SMEARS OF PUDDING

Metamorphic rocks often look like swirls. This lab shows one way that might happen.

MATERIALS

- 4 different pudding mixes or 2 vanilla mixes with 4 food coloring choices—do not use instant pudding
- 4 mixing bowls, with pouring spouts if possible
- Large glass baking dish
- Lazy Susan

 Safety Tips
- Be careful around glass—don't drop it!

PROTOCOL

STEP 1: In the mixing bowls, mix the pudding ingredients according to the package instructions. You can use a mixture of dark chocolate, regular chocolate, butterscotch, and vanilla. If you don't have four packages of pudding, you can make two vanilla mixes and add food coloring to get different colors.

STEP 2: From opposite corners of your dish, quickly pour in two different-colored mixtures. Let them puddle out to halfway across the dish.

STEP 3: Right away, add two more colors from the same places you added them before. Pour slowly so the new pudding mix pushes the previous mix across.

STEP 4: Repeat as long as you have pudding mix, but for no more than five minutes, as pudding usually sets up within that time frame. Try to get nice, even lines in your dish that contrast well with the other mixes.

STEP 5: Before the pudding can set up, grab two opposite corners of the dish and give it a quick shake to one side with a jerk to stop it. This is where a lazy Susan rotating table can come in handy.

STEP 6: At some point, the pudding will set up and you won't get much more action. You can use a spoon or stick to make more swirls, but eventually the pudding is ready to eat!

 Creative Enrichment

1. What happens when great force is applied suddenly?

THE SCIENCE BEHIND THE FUN

Metamorphic rocks like schist and gneiss often resemble the pudding swirls you just created. Such rocks usually get their lines from the original strata in a sedimentary rock, which has been heated and pressurized by the forces in the Earth's crust. But earthquakes must also play a role, because the swirls and folds come in all shapes and sizes. When you gave your rocks a quick shake, you were doing the job of an earthquake.

If you were to keep going, at some point your pudding swirls would probably start to smear and become unrecognizable. Geologists believe the rocks in the Earth's mantle are very hot and probably act like pudding, or melted plastic, and as heat and pressure continue, the rocks change their appearance completely. In the lab Cocoa Crust, you learned about how heat travels through the mantle in convection currents, which can also cause melted rocks to form swirls. There is a lot we don't know about the rocks in the Earth's mantle, but this is a tasty way to learn!

LAB 9

SNAKY SCHIST

If sedimentary rocks are generally flat when they are laid down, how did they get so wavy?

MATERIALS

- 4 slices of yellow cheddar cheese at room temperature
- 4 slices of white cheddar cheese at room temperature

Safety Tips
- Don't make a mess with your cheese, but in this lab, it's okay to play with your food!

PROTOCOL

STEP 1: Take your slices of cheese from the refrigerator. Alternate colors of cheese to neatly stack five slices. Push the edges slightly so a rise appears in the middle. This is an *anticline*. If the bulge dipped down, you would have a *syncline*.

STEP 2: Take your stack apart and put three slices into one neat pile and the other two, plus one new slice, into another. Put the second stack in the refrigerator.

STEP 3: Holding the edges straight, make folds in the cheese by pushing the edges together a little bit at a time. You should see a mound form much easier this time. See how far it can bend without breaking.

STEP 4: Remove the second stack from the refrigerator and immediately repeat the experiment. Don't let the cheese warm up.

STEP 5: Make cheese sandwiches from your leftovers. Making grilled cheese sandwiches will turn the cheese into a metamorphic rock!

 Creative Enrichment

1. Use a thermometer to record the actual temperature of your cheese samples.
2. What would happen if you spread mayonnaise between your layers before you start folding?
3. Try freezing your cheese and see if you can make a single fold. Some rocks are so brittle they don't fold—they fracture.

THE SCIENCE BEHIND THE FUN

When layers of rock get buried at great depths, they stop acting like rocks and start acting like, well, melted cheese. It is much easier to create folds when there is plenty of heat, because the cheese was much easier to bend. As the heat increases, you can almost fold your cheese layers like an accordion.

It should be easier for you to understand what happens not only to rocks the size of your cheese sample, but also to giant slabs of rocks that are heated up and pushed around. Geologists can tell how much heat and pressure a rock has been through by the minerals they find. If a rock gets more heat and pressure, it will become a slate, a common metamorphic rock. It may have started out as a mudstone but has hardly undergone any metamorphism. Next is phyllite, then schist, and finally gneiss, which is very hard.

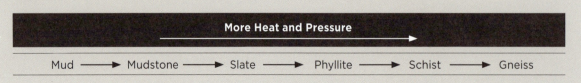

More Heat and Pressure →

Mud → Mudstone → Slate → Phyllite → Schist → Gneiss

LAB 10: CHOCOLATE ROCK CYCLE

Use chocolate to learn about all the different rock cycles.

MATERIALS

- Block or chips of dark chocolate
- Kitchen grater
- Aluminum foil
- Small pot
- 2 cups (475 ml) water
- 4–5 paper cupcake holders
- Block or chips of white chocolate
- Chocolate syrup (optional)

Safety Tips

- Be careful around a hot stove.
- Ask an adult for help using the stove.
- Don't hurt your fingers when you grate up the chocolate.

PROTOCOL

STEP 1: Start by making some "sedimentary" chocolate rock. Take a block of dark chocolate, or large chips—which you can think of as cooled "metamorphic" rock. Use a grater to grate about ¼ cup (44 g) of chocolate powder. This is like the effects of erosion, creating dry sand or mud—the basics of a sedimentary rock.

STEP 2: Create a small "boat" out of aluminum foil and place the powder inside it. Now float the boat in a small pot of water over low heat until you see the powder melt into a liquid chocolate lava flow. This is now "igneous" chocolate.

STEP 3: Pour the hot liquid chocolate lava into a paper cupcake holder and let it cool.

STEP 4: Once cool, break the chocolate into pieces, the way mountains break apart due to erosion. Grate some small shavings from the white chocolate, add it to the broken chocolate pieces, and sprinkle in some chocolate chips or add some chocolate syrup.

STEP 5: Place the mixture of different types of chocolate "rocks" in a small square of aluminum foil, about 8" x 8" (20 x 20 cm). Fold the aluminum foil up by half several times until the chocolate is safely wrapped inside. You can also use sturdy resealable plastic bags.

STEP 6: Place the foil on a flat surface and push on it, but don't use too much force or you could break open the foil. You want enough pressure to press the chocolate particles together—like the amount of force needed to create metamorphic rocks. A light tap with a rubber mallet or a rolling pin would work.

STEP 7: Carefully unwrap the foil and check out the result. You should see a "chocolate schist." By applying a little pressure, and some heat from friction, you forced the chocolate particles to compress together into a metamorphic rock again.

 Creative Enrichment

1. What could you do next to the "metamorphic" chocolate to re-start the cycle?

THE SCIENCE BEHIND THE FUN

Congratulations! You just made a complete cycle through the three main rock types. There is no way to say for sure where rocks start in their journey, so we arbitrarily started with a metamorphic rock and began eroding it. Next, we melted the sedimentary rock and formed volcanic chocolate lava, then we mashed it all together like a metamorphic rock. If your mixture was hard enough, you could start over and begin grating it back into a fine powder. The Earth is a great at recycling rocks. That's the way it happens in the Earth's crust: rocks go through a journey from one form to the next. That's why we say that the Earth is geologically active— these processes are going on all the time.

RESOURCES

Earth Science Week classroom activities
www.earthsciweek.org/classroom-activities
Check here for many more Earth science labs you can do at home.

Identifying rocks online
www.classzone.com, select "Science" as a subject and then click on the "Earth Science" book.
This site helps you identify rocks and minerals based on streak, color, density, and other details.

Kids.gov
kids.usa.gov/teens/science/geology/index.shtml
You'll find many more labs that explain geology and Earth science.

The National Crystal Growing Competition
http://www.cheminst.ca/outreach/crystal-growing-competition
Canadian high school students can grow their own crystals and compete for cash prizes.

ABOUT THE AUTHOR

Garret Romaine has been an avid rock hound, fossil hunter, and gold prospector for 35 years. He is a long-time journalist, columnist, and technical writer who teaches technical writing at Portland State University. He is a Fellow in the Society for Technical Communication, an organization dedicated to explaining complex technology and science. He holds a degree in geology from the University of Oregon and a degree in geography from the University of Washington. He is the author of many books on geology and the outdoors, including *The Modern Rockhounding and Prospecting Handbook, Rockhounding Idaho, Gem Trails of Oregon, Gem Trails of Washington,* and *Gold Panning the Pacific Northwest.* He is a member of the Board of Directors for the Rice Northwest Museum of Rocks and Minerals and also serves on the board of the North American Research Group, devoted to amateur paleontologists.

ACKNOWLEDGMENTS

I'd like to thank photographer Patrick F. Smith for his patience in turning his photography studio into a science laboratory for two months, while we fine-tuned the labs and brought them to life.